GUIDE TO COMPLETE UNDERSTANDING
Preamble to the United States Constitution

Citizens Academy US

No part of this book may be reproduced in any form or by any means, electronic or mechanical, including photocopying, recording, or by any information storage and retrieval system without written permission of the publisher.

Library of Congress Control Number: 2023906249
ISBN: 979-8-9880290-0-7

© 2024 Citizens Academy US. All Rights Reserved

We the People

insure domestic Tranquility, provide for the common
and our Posterity, do ordain and establish this Con

Article I.

Citizens Academy US

"Complete understanding depends upon freedom from misunderstood words."

L. Ron Hubbard

to be best in
point of view

Welcome ['

greet the co

pleasure; s

welcome

Welcome!

There are a tremendous number of conversations happening today about politics and government. They are subjects that many people feel passionate about.

One topic that is now frequently being discussed is the document that founded our government: the United States Constitution.

Many people in the United States have not read this document. And many who have read it, want to understand more about what it means.

L. Ron Hubbard wrote, "Complete understanding depends upon freedom from misunderstood words."

The purpose of the Citizens Academy US is to provide an easy way for all people of the United States to achieve complete understanding of the United States Constitution and the Declaration of Independence.

We don't explain these documents. We don't interpret them. We don't evaluate them.

We simply give you an easy and very enjoyable way to understand them for yourself and to make up your own mind. We do this by giving you the definitions of the words as they were used at the time these documents were written.

Our goal is complete understanding.

Many people have completed this Guide and have written wonderful success stories about learning something new and something they can really use.

They've written that doing The Guide is enlightening and pleasurable. It gave them a new and highly effective way to have conversations with others, even with people they disagree with. Many are enjoying sharing this Guide with others.

We welcome you to try it for yourself!
We look forward to hearing from you!

We welcome you to join us in a new movement to create understanding.

Instructions

You can do The Guide with another person. Many people have told us they really enjoyed pairing up with a partner to do The Guide together while reading out loud and sharing their answers. You can also do The Guide by yourself, or even in a group. The more actively you participate, the more you'll find it meaningful and enjoyable.

If there are any words in the definitions you're not sure of, or if you get curious about any words that aren't defined as you go through The Guide, grab a good dictionary and find the definition that fits the way the word is being used. You can also go online and find the definition in the *American Dictionary of the English Language*, published in 1828, which has the definitions that were used at that time.

You can find that at: https://webstersdictionary1828.com/

The words we use today have been used for many years, going back to ancient times. You'll be learning about where words came from, which will give you a more robust, richer understanding of their meaning.

We would love to hear from you. We would love to hear what you got out of doing The Guide, whether you enjoyed it, any new realizations you had and if it helped you in any way. We're interested in all your thoughts. And please feel free to ask us any questions. This guide is for you! To reach us go to: https://citizensacademy.us/write-us.

Important!

Do the following for each of the words defined in this Guide.

1. Read the definition and the italicized example sentence(s).

2. Take turns telling your learning partner what the definition means in your own words.

3. Take turns with your learning partner giving examples or making up sentences using the word.

Do this until you both know and can use the word very comfortably.

You will experience the real power of The Guide as you give examples and create sentences for each word that's defined. Do this for every word. This way these words will fully come alive for you and you will make them your own. Just reading the definitions will give you a very superficial understanding. Complete understanding will come from giving as many examples and creating as many sentences as you need to feel very comfortable using each word yourself.

Let's Start!

1. Tell your purpose for doing this Guide to your learning partner, if you have one, and find out theirs.

2. Read the Preamble to the United States Constitution (on the next page). Don't worry if you don't fully understand it yet. Just notice how it seems to you now.

3. Next go through each of the definitions, one at a time, following the instructions on the previous page.

We the People

insure domestic Tranquility, provide for the common de[fence]
and our Posterity, do ordain and establish this Constitu[tion]

Section. 1. All legislative Powers herein granted sha[ll]
of Representatives.

Section. 2. The House of Representatives shall be comp[osed]
in each State shall have the Qualifications requisite for Electors of the
No Person shall be a Representative who shall not h[ave]

Preamble

We the People of the United States,

in Order to form a more perfect Union,

establish Justice,

insure domestic Tranquility,

provide for the common Defense,

promote the general Welfare,

and secure the Blessings of Liberty

to ourselves and our Posterity,

do ordain and establish

this Constitution for the United States of America.

The Definitions

We the People

...insure domestic Tranquility, provide for the common...
...and our Posterity, do ordain and establish this Cons[titution]...

Article I

Section 1. All legislative Powers herein granted shall be vested in a Congress of the United States, which shall consist of a Senate and House of Representatives.

Section 2. The House of Representatives shall be composed of Members chosen every second Year by the People of the several States, and the Electors in each State shall have the Qualifications requisite for Electors of the most numerous Branch of the State Legislature.

No Person shall be a Representative who shall not have attained to the Age of twenty five Years, and been seven Years a Citizen of the United States, and who shall not, when elected, be an Inhabitant of that State in which he shall be chosen.

Representatives and direct Taxes shall be apportioned among the several States which may be included within this Union, according to their respective Numbers... and until such enumeration shall be made, ...Connecticut five, New York...

Preamble

The introductory part of a law which states the reasons for and the intent of the law. The preamble sets forth the guiding principles which are intended by the law.

A preamble provides a foundation for the document that follows and prepares the minds of the readers for what comes next. Prepares means to make ready.

The word preamble meant "to walk before" from the Latin words *prae* which meant "before" and *ambulare* which meant "to walk."

•

The preamble of the US Constitution clearly states its six purposes.

We

You together with the
other people you're talking about

All of you

•

We wish you a very happy birthday!

The People

At the time the Preamble was written, all countries in the world were ruled by monarchs (single rulers, one person in charge) which were either a king, queen, emperor or empress.
These monarchs were surrounded by people of the "upper class" who were known as aristocrats or nobles. This was a small group.

The rest of the population, that had no authority and was ruled by these monarchs and aristocrats or nobles, was called "the commoners" or "the people." The term "the people" meant the ordinary persons in a community or nation who did not have any significant social status, and who were not members of royalty, nobility, nor any part of the aristocracy.

(Continued on the next page.)

The People

The words "the people" in the Preamble signify that this document was coming from the people directly, straight from the common, ordinary people, not from or through the rulers, the aristocracy nor any government officials.

Additionally, when you say, "The people," it's different than if you just say, "people." When you put the word "The" in front and say, "The people," it means all the people, or most of the people, in complete agreement, speaking as one voice.

•

The people did not agree with the king's decision and united in protest.

The people want you to be in charge.

The 99% approval vote showed the people want a new library in town.

In order to

So as to make something happen

•

I'm going to leave early in order to be on time.

Form

Bring into being

Create something new

•

She formed a beautiful vase with her hands.

They formed a new organization.

Perfect

Ideal

Lacking nothing

The word perfect comes from the word *perficio* which meant "to complete, to carry to the end."

•

Having you come will make our party even more perfect.

Union

Two or more things joined into one

The word union came from the
word *unus* which meant "one."

•

Their marriage was a true union.

The union of our two businesses makes us both stronger.

Establish

Put there to last a very long time

To make something firm and stable so it operates well on a permanent or very enduring basis

The word establish came from *stabilis* which meant "firm, secure."

•

The Olympic Games were established very well by the ancient Greeks.

He established a great reputation for customer service.

Justice

Giving to everyone what is their due or owed to them,
no more and no less

Making sure people are treated fairly

Rewards and penalties which are applied
when they are deserved and are fair

The word justice came from the word *iustis* which meant
"true, proper, perfect, complete."

•

Justice protects individuals from unfair treatment.

The criminal was caught and faced justice.

Insure

Guarantee there is no possibility of loss

Make safe from risk

The word insure came from the word *ensuren* which meant "make secure, make safe."

•

This will insure our privacy.

We want to insure the power of the citizens.

Domestic

Of this country

Within our borders

The word domestic came from *domus* which meant "house."

•

We have domestic and foreign policy.

This airline is domestic, they don't fly to other countries outside the USA.

Tranquility

Continuing, enduring peace and serenity, calmness

Freedom from turbulence, agitation, chaos, violence, or upset

The word tranquility came from the word *tranquillus* which meant "quiet, calm, still."

•

He wanted to raise his family in the tranquility of a nice, safe neighborhood.

The tranquility of the forest calmed her mind.

Provide

To supply, to furnish with

The word provide came from *providere* which meant "look ahead and see what you'll need."

•

Her father provided her a very good lunch.

Common

Belonging to everyone, owned or used by all

The word common came from *communis* which meant "belonging to all, shared by all."

•

We need to think about the common good.

This is a common park that everyone can use.

Defense

Anything that keeps people free from any harm, danger or trouble

Shields from attack

Defeats aggressors

The word defense came from two words, *de* which meant "completely" and *fendere* which meant "keep off, guard, protect."

•

Eating healthy food is a good defense against getting sick.

Promote

Contribute to its progress

To make larger

To make it grow or increase

The word promote came from *promovere* which meant "move forward."

•

Friendliness promotes good communication.

A nice downtown area promotes the success of all businesses.

We the People of the United States, in Order to form a more perfect Union, establish Justice, insure domestic Tranquility, provide for the common defence, promote the general Welfare, and secure the Blessings of Liberty to ourselves and our Posterity, do ordain and establish this Constitution for the United States of America.

Article. I.

Section. 1. All legislative Powers herein granted shall be vested in a Congress of the United States, which shall consist of a Senate and House of Representatives.

Section. 2. The House of Representatives shall be composed of Members chosen every second Year by the People of the several States, and the Electors in each State shall have the Qualifications requisite for Electors of the most numerous Branch of the State Legislature.

No Person shall be a Representative who shall not have attained to the Age of twenty five Years, and been seven Years a Citizen of the United States, and who shall not, when elected, be an Inhabitant of that State in which he shall be chosen.

Representatives and direct Taxes shall be apportioned among the several States which may be included within this Union, according to their respective Numbers, which shall be determined by adding to the whole Number of free Persons, including those bound to Service for a Term of Years, and excluding Indians not taxed, three fifths of all other Persons. The actual Enumeration shall be made within three Years after the first Meeting of the Congress of the United States, and within every subsequent Term of ten Years, in such Manner as they shall by Law direct. The Number of Representatives shall not exceed one for every thirty Thousand, but each State shall have at Least one Representative; and until such enumeration shall be made, the State of New Hampshire shall be entitled to chuse three, Massachusetts eight, Rhode-Island and Providence Plantations one, Connecticut five, New-York six, New Jersey four, Pennsylvania eight, Delaware one, Maryland six, Virginia ten, North Carolina five, South Carolina five, and Georgia three.

General

For the whole community or nation

For all, for everyone

The word general comes from the word *generalis* which meant "as a whole."

•

Let's consider the general good.

We need a general library everyone will like.

Welfare

Happiness, health and prosperity

The word welfare came from the word *welfaren* which meant "get along abundantly."

•

The welfare of his children was very important to him.

*Businesses prospered in the town,
increasing the welfare of the whole community.*

Secure

Ensure nothing bad happens

Keep from danger or threat

Keep it in place, keep it from being damaged or lost

The word secure came from two words, *se* and *cura*
which meant "free from" and "care."

•

Let's secure the boat to the dock.

The campers secured their personal belongings from the rain.

Blessings

Sources of happiness

The word blessings came from the word *bledsian* which meant "made holy, give thanks."

•

You are a blessing in my life.

My children are a blessing.

I am grateful for all my blessings.

I wish you many blessings.

Freedom

Absence of all restraint and all restrictions

The word freedom comes from *freo*
which meant "acting of one's own will."

•

The animals in the forest enjoyed their freedom.

Liberty

The state of being
free from
oppressive restrictions
from government
on one's way of life, behavior,
belief or political views

*"Oppressive" rules or regulations
would be ones that are too severe,
cruel, harsh, or that limit or
restrict you too much.*

(Continuted on the next page.)

Liberty

Assumes restraints are essential

Control that you DO agree with, that you consider REASONABLE, that you do CONSENT to

The word liberty came from the word *liber* which meant "free."

•

The people enjoyed their liberty after escaping the cruel king.

America is often called "The Land of Liberty."

To Ourselves

Attached to you together with all the
other people you are talking about

The word ourselves came from the word *ure*
which meant "belonging to us."

•

We secured the line to ourselves before we climbed the rock.

We secured these privileges to ourselves.

Posterity

All the future generations that come after us
All of our children, and their children's children,
and their children's children . . .

The word posterity came from *posteritatum*
which meant "future children."

•

Our actions today are our gift to posterity.

Ordain

To give someone or something
special power, authority, or right

Invest with a special power

The word ordain came from *ordinare* which meant
"put in a certain order,
establish something that will continue in a certain order."

•

We ordained this contract by signing it.

The two countries ordained their peace treaty in a signing ceremony.

Constitute

Define what it is and give formal,
binding, and valid existence to

The word constitute came from two words, *com* + *statuere* which meant "caused to stand firmly, unshakable."

•

*The town constituted a committee to
promote the welfare of the townspeople.*

*The organization constituted its Board (group of people) of Advisors
to advise and guide them.*

Constitution

The most senior (possessing the highest power and authority, highest in rank) laws, policies and regulations

Establishes the form of government in a country, state, or kingdom

A document in which the rights, powers, duties, and responsibilities of citizens and public officials are defined, and how decisions will be made

Determines what future laws will be legal and which will not be allowed, limits and controls the power of the government

The word constitution comes from two words, *com* + *statuere* which meant "caused to stand firmly, unshakable."

•

The Constitution allows anyone to be elected President of the United States as long as they are at least 35 years of age, a natural born citizen (US citizen at birth), and they've lived in the United States for at least 14 years.

The US Constitution contains a process for making changes to the Constitution, and these are called "amendments."

Unite

To cause all powers and efforts
to join together as one

The word unite came from the word *unus* which meant "one."

•

They were united by a passionate purpose to see their sports team win the championship.

The states of North America united to form one nation.

State

A group of people occupying a defined territory and united by one government

The word state came from the word *sta* which meant "to stand and be firm."

•

The state of Ohio is known for the Rock and Roll Hall of Fame.

The people of our state voted to make the Mountain Bluebird the official state bird. (Idaho)

We the People

...insure domestic Tranquility, provide for the common de[fence]... and our Posterity, do ordain and establish this Constitut[ion]...

Article. I.

Section. 1. All legislative Powers herein granted shall [be vested in a Congress of the United States, which shall consist of a Senate and House] of Representatives.

Section. 2. The House of Representatives shall be comp[osed of Members chosen every second Year by the People of the several States, and the Electors] in each State shall have the Qualifications requisite for Electors of th[e most numerous Branch of the State Legislature.]

No Person shall be a Representative who shall not ha[ve...]

Read the *Preamble* to the *United States Constitution* out loud.

Preamble

We the People of the United States,
in Order to form a more perfect Union,
establish Justice,
insure domestic Tranquility,
provide for the common Defense,
promote the general Welfare,
and secure the Blessings of Liberty
to ourselves and our Posterity,
do ordain and establish
this Constitution for the United States of America.

Share Your New Understanding

1. Take turns with your learning partner sharing your understanding, telling each other what the Preamble means to you. Do this until you both feel very good about it.

2. Tell your learning partner what you learned and any wins or realizations you had while doing this Guide.

3. We would love to hear from you. We would love to hear what you got out of doing The Guide, whether you enjoyed it, any new realizations you had and if it helped you in any way. We're interested in all your thoughts. And please feel free to ask us any questions. This guide is for you! To reach us go to: https://citizensacademy.us/write-us.

4. If you are interested in helping others learn about The Guide, let us know and we will send you simple instructions.
Go to: https://citizensacademy.us/write-us.

"Words are not just a dry academic subject. They carry the tide* of progressing civilization."

L. Ron Hubbard

*Carry the tide – Impel, drive or urge forward

Find Out More!

For more information and to purchase hardcover and softcover copies of this Guide go to:

www.citizensacademy.us

L. Ron Hubbard

About L. Ron Hubbard

The Citizens Academy US uses discoveries by L. Ron Hubbard regarding the importance of knowing and using the correct definitions of words in order to achieve full comprehension and understanding.

The life of best-selling American author and educator L. Ron Hubbard reflects his dedication to education. Throughout his life he sought to help others learn.

His systematic research into the problems in education resulted in his discovery of the barriers that make learning a challenge, and with that, the discovery of effective solutions.

L. Ron Hubbard firmly believed that true education was not a matter of memorization, but rather of learning how to acquire and use knowledge in the pursuit of one's goals.

L. Ron Hubbard engaged in many research projects which included such diverse topics as successful management practices, leadership, strategic planning, photography, art and even religious philosophy.

While L. Ron Hubbard wrote extensively on these other topics, they are outside the scope of Citizens Academy US. Our materials are based solely on his breakthrough articles and lectures in the field of effective education.

Appied Scholastics Campus
(aerial view)

Applied Scholastics International
11755 Riverview Dr.
St. Louis, MO, 63138
United States
Phone: 314-355-6355
Toll free: 877-75-LEARN
E-mail: education@appliedscholastics.org

Applied Scholastics International

Citizens Academy US is licensed by Applied Scholastics to use L. Ron Hubbard's breakthrough learning methodology to create educational materials that help individuals fully understand the most important documents of our country.

Applied Scholastics trains educators, teachers and students at all levels and from all over the world on this breakthrough learning methodology.

Applied Scholastics works with schools, home-schoolers, community leaders, civic groups and others to bring about effective education.

Educators utilizing these breakthroughs teach individuals how to learn and master any subject with full comprehension and ability to apply it to their lives, enabling them to achieve their full potential.

Applied Scholastics has the vision to create a world free from illiteracy, in which educational standards are raised and effective teaching is the norm. Applied Scholastics envisions a world in which people, empowered by knowing how to study, are able to achieve their goals and improve their lives, thereby creating a new civilization founded upon knowledge and understanding.

© 2024 Citizens Academy US. All rights reserved. Citizens Academy US is licensed to use Applied Scholastics educational services. Applied Scholastics and the Applied Scholastics logo are trademarks and service marks owned by Association for Better Living and Education International and are used with its permission. Grateful acknowledgment is given to L. Ron Hubbard Library for permission to reproduce selections from the copyrighted works of L. Ron Hubbard. Special acknowledgment is made to the L. Ron Hubbard Library for permission to reproduce photographs from his personal collection.

APPLIED SCHOLASTICS®
EDUCATION SERVICES AND MATERIALS
BASED ON THE WORKS OF L. RON HUBBARD